394

"BARMBY MOOR C.E.
SCHOOL PROPERTY
PLEASE RETURN THIS BOOK
AS SOON AS POSSIBLE"

KU-020-144

SPRING FESTIVALS

Mike Rosen

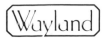

Seasonal Festivals

Autumn Festivals
Winter Festivals
Spring Festivals
Summer Festivals

Cover: Girls selling flowers to celebrate the arrival of spring in Portugal.

Editor: Geraldine Purcell
Designer: Ross George

First published in 1990 by
Wayland (Publishers) Limited
61 Western Road, Hove
East Sussex, BN3 1JD, England

© Copyright 1990 Wayland (Publishers) Limited

British Library Cataloguing in Publication Data
Rosen, Mike 1959–
    Spring festivals.
    1. Festivals
    I. Title II. Series
    394.2

HARDBACK ISBN 1-85210-950-5

PAPERBACK ISBN 0-7502-0941-0

Typeset by Rachel Gibbs, Wayland
Printed by Casterman

Contents

Spring

During the last few weeks of winter, people wait for the first signs of spring. They watch the buds appear on trees and the first flowers bloom in parks and gardens. Out in the fields and woods, animals begin to wake from their winter's hibernation. In cold countries people wait for the warmth of spring, which will thaw the frozen lakes and streams, and change the crisp snow of winter into slush.

Spring is a busy time for farmers as it is the season when many animals give birth. This gives young animals plenty of time to grow strong before the start of the winter. Sheep farmers have to work day and night in all weathers to be sure that their ewes give birth safely, and to protect the young lambs from animals such as foxes. Farmers may also prepare to harvest their winter crops or sow their fields with corn and wheat for the summer.

Above Squirrels store nuts and berries in autumn. This helps them survive when there is little food available in winter and early spring.

Left Seeing lambs playing in fields reminds us that spring has arrived.

Spring is a time when the hardships of winter are past. After the spring equinox, on 21 March in the northern hemisphere, the days begin to last longer than the nights, and nature seems full of energy for growth and new life. Many New Year festivals are held in early spring. Flower festivals celebrate the growth of plants, and there are many joyous occasions which mark the end of winter. Some festivals combine a celebration of new life with a time to remember more serious things – hunger and sorrow, or the death of relatives and friends.

Below **Hedgehogs are one of the species that hibernates during winter to conserve their energy, ready for the mating season in spring.**

April Fools' Day

In Britain the first day of April is known as a time for playing tricks and practical jokes. Children especially like to trick adults. People may find their alarm clocks have been set to wake them at the wrong time, or that their shoelaces have been tied together. Many April Fools' tricks involve telling a person something that sends them on a useless journey – maybe that a shop is giving things free to any customer wearing a green coat. If anyone believes the story and visits the shop dressed in a green coat they can be called an April Fool. It is fun to think up new tricks, but anyone who plays a trick after midday is an April Fool themself.

April Fools' Day carries on an old tradition that people should have a chance to make fun of their rulers on certain days. In ancient Rome, during the feast of Saturnalia, a slave was made Emperor for a day. An old custom of the rulers of some European countries was to make a member of their court the Lord of Misrule. This person had to make sure that everybody at court broke the normal rules of behaviour during the celebrations. In times when rules of behaviour were strict, and breaking them was often punished by death, festivals like April Fools' Day gave people a chance to relax and enjoy themselves. Nobody knows why 1 April was chosen for this festival, but at the start of spring everyone is ready to have fun after the miserable winter weather.

Opposite **The Lord of Misrule encouraged others to have fun and to join in with practical jokes. April Fools' Day carries on these traditions to this day.**

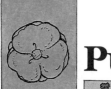

Purim

Left **These Jewish schoolchildren are re-enacting the Purim story.**

Today, in those parts of the world where most people live in warm homes and food is always available, living through the winter does not seem so difficult. The first fall of snow may even seem quite exciting. Elsewhere, the first snow marks the beginning of a time of cold weather for people who may have little fuel to heat their homes, and perhaps have to go hungry if local farmers have had a bad harvest. In the past, most people were used to a hard life and winter was a season to fear. Part of the joy people feel when spring arrives comes from relief that the hardship of winter is over.

The Jewish festival of Purim celebrates this feeling of survival. Jews gather together to hear the story of Queen Esther, a Jewess who was married to Ahasuerus, the ruler of Baghdad many centuries ago. Ahasuerus employed an official called Haman to advise him how to govern. Haman hated the Jews and persuaded Ahasuerus to order the death of all the Jews in Baghdad.

Just before the day set for this massacre, Queen Esther told Ahasuerus that, as she was also Jewish, she too would have to be killed if Haman had his way. Ahasuerus was so angry that he changed the order and hanged Haman instead.

When this story is told the children in the audience hiss and make noises with rattles and drums every time Haman's name is mentioned. After the story has been told, people put on fancy dress and have parties where the children play tricks on the adults.

Left **The Purim festival is an opportunity for people to wear fancy dress and have lots of fun.**

Holi

An ancient Hindu legend tells the story of the struggle between Prahlada and the demon Holika. Prahlada was the son of a demon. However, he refused to worship his evil father, preferring to honour the god Vishnu. The father's sister, Holika, was a demon, and she believed that fire could not harm her. Prahlada's father and Holika decided to use Holika's powers to kill Prahlada. As Holika held Prahlada prisoner in a huge bonfire, the god Vishnu saw what was happening. Before he could be harmed, Vishnu rescued Prahlada from the flames, and the evil demon Holika was burnt to death instead.

This tale is often told as part of the Hindu festival of Holi. In some Indian villages during the festival, mothers carry their young children in a circle around a blazing bonfire.

Below **Everybody enjoys taking part in the paint-throwing and practical jokes of the Hindu festival of Holi.**

Left **Colourful pretend battles are part of the Sikh festival of Hola Mohalla.**

They believe this will help to protect the children from danger in the coming year.

Holi is also a time when people can forget their normal rules of behaviour. At this time of the year everyone is equal. Practical jokes and tricks can be played without any fear of punishment. One tradition is for groups of men or women to run round the streets spraying each other with coloured paints or powder, which wash out easily when the festival is over. This custom grew from the ancient tale of the god Krishna's visit to Earth, when he played such games with young women as they herded their cows.

At the same time as the Hindus celebrate Holi, many Sikhs hold their own festival of Hola Mohalla. During this celebration there are sports competitions and pretend battles, as well as feasts. However, there is no paint throwing or practical jokes such as those enjoyed by the Hindus during Holi.

Below **An illustration of Krishna joining in with the paint-throwing games.**

11

Pesah

Pesah is a Jewish festival which mixes joyful celebration with a time to remember past sorrows. Originally Pesah was mainly a spring harvest festival, but for many centuries Jews have used it to celebrate how their God helped them escape from slavery in Egypt during the reign of the Pharaohs.

During the week of Pesah, Jews think about the importance of freedom for themselves and for all people. They give thanks for events which have brought more freedom, and promise to live in ways that help freedom to grow. Some Jews feel this to be their duty to a God who works to free all humans, while others see it as their part in trying to make the world a better place to live in.

The main part of the Pesah celebrations is a

Above **This illustration shows the Egyptians drowning in the Red Sea after Moses had led the Israelites to safety. Pesah is the time Jews celebrate being led to freedom by Moses.**

meal called Seder. (The word seder means 'order'.) To remind themselves of the pain of slavery, people eat a bitter food, such as radish, with matzah, a dry hard bread that has been made without yeast so that it does not rise into a soft loaf. (When the Jews fled Egypt there was no time to make bread with yeast as it would have taken too long to rise.) Then the bitter food is eaten with a sweet paste made from apple, nuts, honey, wine and spice. There may also be hard-boiled eggs which are dipped in salt water before they are eaten. This part of the meal reminds everyone that joy can come after sorrow in the same way that freedom came after slavery for their ancestors. In this way people are also reminded that after winter comes the new life of spring.

Below **Pesah is an important Jewish celebration when the whole family gathers together for the Seder meal.**

Flower Festivals

One of the clearest signs of spring is the appearance of new buds on the branches of trees and the blooming of flowers such as daffodils and tulips. In many schools children grow daffodils and other flowers in small pots. Daffodils are an important part of the Welsh festival of St David's Day which is celebrated on 1 March. Although this festival remembers a Christian saint, its origins lie in the ancient Celtic celebrations of the end of winter. On St David's Day many Welsh people wear a daffodil or a leek pinned to their clothes. This spring flower and winter vegetable mark the passing of winter into spring.

Later in the spring there are flower festivals in many parts of the world. The most famous

Above **There are many beautiful flower-festivals held in India, such as this colourful festival in Bangalore.**

14

of these are held in the Netherlands, where the tulip fields are a blaze of colour in late April. There are parades of floats decorated with flowers in many towns. Towards the end of May the Chelsea Flower Show is held in London. When this was first opened in 1913 it was called the Great Spring Show. Today it is a huge exhibition which contains many new varieties of plants and ideas for designing beautiful gardens.

Some of the most beautiful spring flowers in the world are the blossoms of the cherry tree. In early April, delicate pink and white flowers decorate these trees and lie scattered across the ground where the wind has blown them. In Japan, people like to walk or picnic in the parks at this time to celebrate the beauty of spring.

Below **Japanese people celebrate the Cherry Blossom Festival by having picnics in parks.**

The History of Easter

Easter is one of the most important festivals of the year for Christians. At this time, they remember the crucifixion of Jesus Christ and his Resurrection three days later. Christians believe that Christ died so that the people of the world could make a new start in their lives, forgiven by God for any wrong actions or thoughts. In this way Easter is linked to other spring festivals which, although they might not be based on any religion, celebrate a new start for the world after the end of winter.

Easter customs often reflect the older festivals they grew out of. The people who lived in northern Europe before the growth of Christianity held a spring festival in honour of their goddess Eostre, who was a goddess of life and birth. In France the festival of Easter is

Below **This is part of an Easter procession through the streets of Margoa in Goa.**

called Pâques, while in Italy it is called
Pasqua. These names, similar to Pesah,
remind us that the first Christians were Jews
who celebrated the Resurrection of Christ as
part of Pesah.

Eggs are an important part of the Pesah
meal called Seder. Throughout the world they
are regarded as a symbol of new life. Eggs
decorated with brightly painted patterns are a
traditional part of the Easter festival. Today,
children in many countries receive chocolate
eggs as part of the Easter celebrations. In
Germany chocolate hares are given instead.
Because it is always full of energy in the
spring, the hare was said to be the favourite
animal of the ancient goddess Eostre.

Above **The
traditional Easter
gifts of painted
eggs and
chocolate hares
are connected
more with the
new spring
season than with
a Christian
festival.**

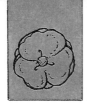

Easter Celebrations

Easter lasts one week, beginning on Palm Sunday and ending on Easter Sunday. This is called Holy Week. It was on Palm Sunday that Christians believe Jesus entered Jerusalem, greeted by crowds waving branches of palm trees. Today, on Palm Sunday some churches are decorated with branches of trees showing the green leaves of spring.

During Holy Week some churches hold readings of the Gospels – stories of Jesus' life. On Maundy Thursday the church is often specially cleaned and the altar is washed. This commemorates the Last Supper when Jesus

Above **The shrine of Our Lady of Sorrows is decorated with fresh flowers and carried through Seville in Spain in the Holy Week processions.**

Left **A Palm Sunday procession in Jerusalem marks the beginning of Holy Week.**

18

washed his disciples' feet to show them that leaders should not think they are more important than anyone else. Nowadays, some Roman Catholic priests may re-enact this.

Christians believe it was on Good Friday that Jesus was crucified. In some places Christians remember this day by performing special plays about the events of Holy Week. These are called Passion Plays and are often performed in beautiful costumes.

On Easter Sunday Christians gather in church to celebrate the day when Jesus was Resurrected. In some countries people attend church just before midnight on Saturday, waiting silently in the darkness for the beginning of the new day. As the church bells sound the start of Sunday, the priest will light a candle and say, 'Christ is risen'. The crowd answer by lighting their own candles and the church is suddenly filled with light instead of darkness.

Left **Easter parades, such as this one in London, are popular events, with brightly decorated floats and people wearing fancy dress costumes.**

Ch'ing Ming

While many festivals celebrate spring as a time of new life, many other people choose this season to remember their friends and family members who have died. In the traditions of the Chinese religion, when a person dies their spirit lives on. If spirits are unhappy they will cause trouble for those still living. For this reason burial sites are chosen carefully and members of the same family are buried close to each other.

At Ch'ing Ming, burial sites are tidied and memorials are cleaned. Then a meal is eaten at the graveside. The food is normally prepared the day before Ch'ing Ming and is eaten cold. Before the meal begins, tea or wine

Above **The burning of paper offerings during Ch'ing Ming, at a grave in Guangdong, China.**

20

is poured on the ground around the grave so that the spirits may also drink. Then, after a portion of food has been set aside for the spirits, the family celebrate with a picnic.

After the meal a ceremony is often held, at which pieces of paper representing money, clothes, or other useful things are burnt by the grave. Anything that is burnt is believed to be received by the ancestral spirits and will increase their wealth and happiness.

After this ceremony, many people spend the rest of the day flying kites. Chinese kites come in many different shapes and sizes – fish, birds, dragons and lions are all popular designs. As evening falls, candles are placed inside the kites which then glow in the dark, their little lights twisting and turning in wild patterns.

Below **A colourful and dramatic Chinese dragon kite.**

New Year Festivals

With so many spring festivals celebrating the renewal of life after winter, it is not surprising that some people choose to celebrate the beginning of their new year at the time of the spring equinox.

One of the oldest religions in the world is Zoroastrianism, which was founded in Persia (Iran), early in the sixth century BC. For thousands of years Zoroastrians followed a calendar which contained 365 days. Because this is a slightly shorter period than the solar year, they found that the dates of their festivals were gradually moving away from their original seasons. Early in the twentieth century a group of Zoroastrians, called Parsis, adopted the Gregorian calendar, which

Left To welcome in the New Year, branches from evergreen trees and food have been placed at the entrance of this house in Goa during No Ruz.

matches the solar year exactly. They decided to place their New Year festival, No Ruz, at the spring equinox on 21 March.

Parsis celebrate No Ruz with great joy. In the morning people give each other presents and everyone wears new clothes. There are special foods for breakfast before a visit to the temple for prayers. Houses may be decorated with branches from evergreen trees. Throughout the day people visit each other for celebration parties.

The Baha'i New Year is also called No Ruz and falls on 21 March. The Baha'i religion teaches that worship should not become a fixed routine. For this reason there are no set ways of celebrating any Baha'i festival, but there is usually a meal at which followers eat together in large groups, and it is a time to offer prayers together.

Above **No Ruz is the first Holy Day of the Baha'i calendar.**

Baisakhi

Sikhs and some Hindus celebrate the start of their new year in the middle of April, which in India falls towards the end of spring. At this time the winter crops are fully grown. Baisakhi is a New Year festival which is also used to celebrate an early harvest.

The Baisakhi festival in 1699 saw the beginning of a vital tradition of the Sikh religion. At a large meeting, the Guru Gobind Singh called for volunteers to die for their religion. In turn, five men disappeared into a tent with the Guru, who later came out carrying a bloodstained sword. The crowd believed the five men were dead, but they then emerged from the tent unharmed and dressed in robes of yellow silk. The Guru made them promise to follow five new rules for the Sikh religion. In return they, and anyone else in the crowd who made the same promise, would be especially honoured by all Sikhs as members of the Khalsa, which means 'pure ones'.

Nowadays, Sikhs celebrate the religious festival of Baisakhi with prayers at their temple. It is usual for young people to go through a ceremony to join the Khalsa. Afterwards there may be discussions about religion or politics and there is often a special meal followed by dancing. In the Indian countryside the dances are often performed in the fields. Dressed in bright costumes, both men and women dance to celebrate the harvest and the new year.

Opposite **The two men in yellow robes are members of the Khalsa. The Khalsa or 'pure ones' are a brotherhood of Sikhs pledged to defend and uphold their faith.**

Buddhist New Year

Buddhism began in northern India and some Buddhists use a calendar based on the ancient Indian one, which places New Year in mid-April. In Thailand, Buddhists celebrate their New Year between 13 and 15 April with a festival called Songkran. As the Thai New Year falls at the start of the South-east Asian hot dry season, water plays an important part in its celebration. Statues of the Buddha are carefully bathed, and after this ceremony people throw water over each other until everyone is soaking wet. There are boat races, parades, plays and concerts.

Similar celebrations take place in Burma, though New Year takes place a few days later

Above **This woman, at a Thai temple, is adding gold-leaf to the statue as a New Year offering to Buddha.**

26

than in Thailand – on 16 or 17 April. In Burma water throwing is just one of many practical jokes and tricks which people may play on each other. In this way the Burmese New Year festival is similar to April Fools' Day or Holi. For one day of the year, the rules of behaviour are forgotten and nobody should become angry at being the victim of a soaking or a trick.

In Sri Lanka New Year falls on 13 April. People visit their family and friends, and give each other gifts. As in Thailand there are festivals of dance and music at this time. Amongst all the noise and celebration people try to find time to think about the past year, and especially to forgive anyone who may have hurt or harmed them, so that the new year can start free from anger.

Below **The wonderful spectacle of New Year fireworks over the temples at Ayutthaya, the old capital of Thailand.**

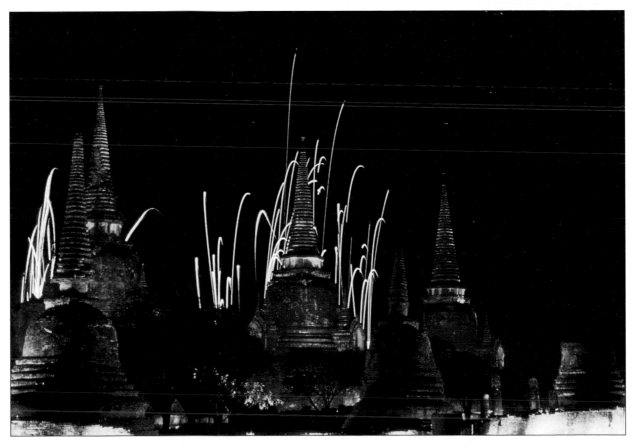

The Apoo Festival

Apoo is a New Year festival celebrated in Ghana which lasts thirteen days, ending the day after the spring equinox. On each of the first eleven days of Apoo, different dances are performed; some to drive away evil, some to honour ancestral spirits, and some to bring good fortune and a rich harvest in the new year. On the twelfth day of Apoo the shrines of the spirits are taken in a procession down to a river where they are washed, so they may end the old year free from the memory of any bad events.

Apoo ends with a ceremony to welcome the new year. When the festival was celebrated mainly in country villages, these ceremonies

Below **Ghanaian women dress in their finery for every festival.**

Above **Ghanaian festivals are lively and happy occasions.**

included the killing of animals as sacrifices to the spirits. Today many of those villages have grown into towns, and the sacrifice of animals has been replaced by offerings of specially cooked vegetables such as yams.

Apoo celebrations are, in one way, similar to other spring festivals such as April Fools' Day and Holi. People can say what they like about each other without fear of punishment. Traditionally people speak out about the behaviour of their government or make fun of important and powerful people, but Apoo is also a chance for people to make public any complaint they have against another person. By talking about their problems in public, people can settle their arguments and enter the new year in friendship.

Glossary

Celtic The Celts were people who lived in Europe and Britain in pre-Roman times.

Crucifixion A form of execution used by the ancient Romans. It involved nailing a person to a cross and leaving them to hang there until they died. It is believed that this is the way that Christ was executed.

Equinox The two times of year, in spring and autumn, when the hours of daylight equal the hours of night-time.

Evergreen The word used to describe those plants which continue to bear leaves, fruit, or berries through the winter.

Ewes Female sheep.

Gregorian Calendar This calendar was named after Pope Gregory XIII, who introduced its use in 1582. The Gregorian calendar adds one day to the length of the year once every four years. This brought the calendar into line with the solar year which is actually 365¼ days long.

Guru A wise and important teacher. The Sikh religion acknowledges the teachings of ten gurus.

Hibernation The method by which some mammals survive winter. It is a deep sleep during which the body saves energy to keep the vital organs like the heart and the brain working.

Legend An ancient story, often telling of important historical events.

Massacre The killing of a large number of people.

Pharaohs The title given to the rulers of ancient Egypt.

Resurrection Rising from the dead. Christians believe that after Christ died on the cross he was Resurrected before going up to heaven.

Shrine A sacred place where people worship a particular god, goddess, or other object of devotion. A shrine can also be a chest or cabinet, built to hold religious relics.

Solar A word used to describe anything related to the sun.

Books to Read

These books might be of interest to you. You can get them through your local library. Ask the librarian to help you to find them.

Buddhist Festivals, by J Snelling (Wayland, 1985)
Easter, by J Fox (Wayland, 1984)
Festivals and Celebrations, by R Purton (Basil Blackwell,1983)
Festivals and Customs, by N J Bull (A Wheaton, 1979)

Festivals Around the World, by P Steele (Macmillian, 1983)
Hindu Festivals, by S Mitter (Wayland, 1985)
India Celebrates, by J W Watson (Garrard, Illinois, 1974)
Jewish Festivals, by R Turner (Wayland, 1985)
Sikh Festivals, by S S Kapoor (Wayland, 1985)
Spring, by D Lambert (Wayland, 1986)

Picture Acknowledgements

The publishers would like to thank the following for allowing their pictures to be reproduced:

David Bowden Photo Library 21; Chapel Studios 14; C M Dixon 12; Eye Ubiquitous 16, 22, 23, 25; Format Photographers 29; Jimmy Holmes 20; The Hutchison Library 10, 11 (left), 15, 28; Frank Lane Agency 4 (left); The Mansell Collection 7; Christine Osborne Pictures 26, 27; Ann & Bury Peerless 11 (right); Tony Stone Worldwide 4 (right), 5; Topham Picture Library 18 (right), 19; ZEFA 8, 9, 13, 17, 18 (left). All artwork is by Maggie Downer. Cover ZEFA.

Index